TWENTY FUN DEVOTIONS FROM
PROVERBS

"It's Our Time, Dad"

20 FUN DEVOTIONS FROM

PROVERBS

GREG JOHNSON

Tyndale House Publishers, Inc.
WHEATON, ILLINOIS

Interior illustrations copyright © 1994 by
Bron Smith

Scripture quotations are taken from the
Holy Bible, New International Version®.
Copyright © 1973, 1978, 1984 by
International Bible Society. Used by
permission of Zondervan Publishing
House. All rights reserved. The "NIV"
and "New International Version"
trademarks are registered in the United
States Patent and Trademark Office by
International Bible Society. Use of either
trademark requires permission of
International Bible Society.

Library of Congress Catalog Card
Number 94-60986
ISBN 0-8423-1747-3

Printed in the United States of America

99 98 97 96 95 94
 7   6   5   4   3   2   1

**To
Troy and Drew,
that
you may know
Jesus—
and me.**

*He will turn
the hearts
of the fathers
to their children,
and the hearts
of the children
to their fathers.*
Malachi 4:6

Dads, Read This

Yes, it's tough to find the time to work on a book like this with your child, but the few total hours it will take to complete could pay dividends for years to come. Once you get started, you probably won't even have to coax or remind your child it's time to do another section. Why? Because with all of the rewards built in, they'll want to complete it—fast! Your child can earn points for completing various sections of each fun devotion. As their points add up, they can cash them in for prizes—things the two of you have agreed on in advance. (See page 4 for a list of suggested prizes. Feel free to customize this list by adding things of special interest to your child and you.)

But don't go too fast through each devotion. Make sure they understand each passage. Most importantly, get ready to take a trip down memory lane. You'll find yourself recalling things about your own grade-school days you thought you'd forgotten years ago. When you're done with this book, your child will know exactly what you were like when you were his or her age!

How Long Should It Take You to Get through This Book?

There's no set amount of time. It should take ten to twenty minutes per chapter. Don't feel rushed—and don't rush. Let the lessons sink in, and help your child apply what you're learning.

Finally, though each section should relate to any child in third through sixth grade, feel free to skip a chapter or two if your kids can't relate to the subject. That will just get them to the rewards a little faster! Or, if you're finding that most of the lessons don't apply, put the book aside for a year or two until they do.

Kids, Read This

You're about to take an adventure through the book of Proverbs.

OK, so it probably won't be as fun as Walt Disney World. But what's fun about this adventure is that you get to take your dad with you. You can't do it alone. Along the way, as you and he complete a number of sections, you'll earn points for prizes and rewards!

The goal of this book is for you and your dad to go through selected passages from Proverbs together, find out what they say, and especially what they mean. Your dad will be asking you some questions—some will be easy; others will require a little thought. But hey, you're up for a challenge, aren't you?

Another goal is for you to learn what your dad was like when he was your age. Does he tell you stories about when he was a kid? If he doesn't, he will now! Feel free to ask him a lot of questions on how he handled each situation. You'll learn a lot!

How fast you go through this book is up to you and your dad. When you're done with each lesson and section, mark it off in the front of the book so you can check how close you are to the next reward! You're the scorekeeper in this adventure!

The best time to remind Dad to sit down with you alone is probably after dinner or right before bed. You set the schedule with him so it works out best for both of you.

Are you ready? Then grab a pencil while Dad reads the rules—and then get going!

The Rules of the Game

Before you get started, Dad, let's talk about how you're supposed to be doing each lesson:

It's Alive: You or your child can read the passage. It doesn't matter who does it.

Let's Dig: Ask your child these questions. Some require thought, some are the yes-and-no variety, and some invite you to help your child find the answer. If your child gets stuck on any of them, either answer them yourself or move on to the next one. Some questions may be over the heads of second or third graders, but hopefully not too many.

Dad's Turn: This is where your child asks you the questions. The goal is for you to try to remember *stories* and *feelings* you had as a grade-schooler. If you honestly can't relate to the question or can't remember a situation, move on to the next one. If other stories come to mind that almost relate to the topic, tell them. Talking about your past is the goal.

What If . . . : It's your child's turn to answer again. You read the situation, making sure your child understands what's happening, then ask the questions. Sometimes there's one situation, sometimes more. If you're good at thinking up "What If" situations and you can think of something that may apply better to your child, then by all means use it.

Now What? This may be the most important part: application. Now's your chance to teach your child the life skill of learning how to apply passages from the Bible. Again, if what's written doesn't help your child apply the passage, think of something else that will.

Overtime Challenge: If you have enough time (and your child wants to earn bonus points), open your Bible, read the passages, and answer the questions. This should help shed some more light on the opening verses and generate more discussion.

Plant It Deep or **Pray It Up:** Some sections end with a verse to memorize, others with a prayer to pray. The memorization is optional, but again, your child will earn extra points (and more rewards) by doing it. If your time has run out, both of you can memorize it separately at a later time, then recite it before the next section to still get credit. After you're done, you can review each memorized verse to earn extra points. You don't have to be word perfect on the passages unless that's what you agree to. (A good compromise is to allow three "hints.")

Puzzles: After every five lessons there's either a crossword puzzle or a word search. The crosswords are fairly easy, the word searches could take some time. If you've got all but a couple of words, that's close enough. Just have fun doing the puzzles together.

Can This Book Be Used for Family Devotions?

Sure! If your children are close together in age—and Mom wants to be involved—go for it. All you have to do is make some decisions about how the points are kept (or perhaps not kept at all). Then, when you ask the questions for kids and read the "What If" situations, try to get everyone to respond. Then when it's "Dad's Turn," have Mom answer too. Not every question will apply to her, but that's OK. Just try to keep the lesson moving so the kids don't get bored.

Suggested Prize Lists

These are only suggestions for prizes. If a prize is too expensive to offer, the parent has the option to choose different prizes . . . as long as the child agrees to them, of course!

PRIZE LIST "A" (for 1,500 points or more)
- Have ice cream some weekday evening with just you and Dad.
- Rent a video and watch it together.
- Take a trip to the local library to look for some great books.
- Have lunch at a favorite fast-food spot.
- Go through old photo albums together and make a

collage of pictures of just you two to put in a special wall hanging.

- Go buy a model and put it together.
- Walk to the store together to buy some junk food.
- Shoot hoops for an hour.
- Learn a new board game.
- Take a long drive.
- Make breakfast together for the whole family.
- Learn a new card game.
- Go to Dairy Queen for a Mister Misty.
- Your choice: _____
- Your choice: _____
- Your choice: _____

PRIZE LIST "B" (for 2,500 points or more)
- Buy two packs of premium sports cards.
- Go to the toy store and buy a new game to play together.
- Go to the Christian bookstore together, listen to some new tapes, and pick out the one you want.
- Go see a movie.
- Go play miniature golf together.
- Learn how to play tennis.
- Go on an all-day hike.
- Work on a project together in the garage (birdhouse, bookcase, Christmas decoration, etc.).
- Start a new collection.
- Take a trip to the zoo. (Maybe he'll take the whole family!)
- Your choice: _____
- Your choice: _____
- Your choice: _____

PRIZE LIST "C" (for 5,000 points or more)
- Go on a long bike ride and picnic with Dad.
- Dad takes you on a fifteen-dollar shopping spree at the local mall.
- Have pizza and play games at Chuck E Cheese's.
- Go bowling together once a month for three straight months.

- Take a trip to a sports card show with fifteen dollars from Dad.
- Skip church and go for a drive (just kidding).
- Make a fort or a playhouse.
- Your choice: _____
- Your choice: _____
- Your choice: _____

PRIZE LIST "D" (for 10,000 points or more)
- Your allowance gets raised by fifty cents a week for a whole year.
- Go on a day fishing trip with Dad.
- Have breakfast with Dad once a month for six months at a favorite breakfast spot.
- Go to a pro sports game together (getting there early enough to watch them practice).
- Go camping together for one night and day.
- Your choice: _____
- Your choice: _____
- Your choice: _____

PRIZE LIST "E" (for 15,000 points or more)
- Your allowance gets raised by one dollar a week for a whole year.
- Go on an overnight fishing trip with Dad.
- Go camping with Dad for two days.
- Buy a new Bible Nintendo game.
- Buy new tennis shoes or an outfit that you've wanted.
- Take six weeks of golf or tennis lessons together (depending on the price).
- Go snow skiing together for the day.
- Buy a new Game Boy cartridge.
- Your choice: _____
- Your choice: _____
- Your choice: _____

POINT TOTALS

Section One	Done Points	Bonus Points	Total
1. The Father Who Loves	500	_300_	_800_
2. Safe and Secure	500	_____	_____
3. Where Do You Find Happiness?	500	_____	_____
4. A Good Choice	500	_____	_____
5. Master the Motive	500	_____	_____
Add Puzzle Points			_____
Grand Total			_____
Subtract Points Redeemed			_____
Points to Be Carried Over			_____

7 ~

Section Two	Done Points	Bonus Points	Total
6. Is Every Pal a Friend?	500	_____	_____
7. A Helping Hand	500	_____	_____
8. Who Made the "Target"?	500	_____	_____
9. Giving Courage	500	_____	_____
10. It Rots the Bones	500	_____	_____
Add Puzzle Points			_____
Add Carry-over Points from Section 1			_____
Grand Total			_____
Subtract Points Redeemed			_____
Points to Be Carried Over			_____

Section Three	Done Points	Bonus Points	Total
11. You Give, He Takes, Everyone Wins!	500	_____	_____
12. To Work or Not to Work?	500	_____	_____
13. Every Dad's Nightmare	500	_____	_____
14. To Be Patient, or Not to Be, That Is the Question	500	_____	_____
15. Are You Vinegar Smoke?	500	_____	_____
Add Puzzle Points			_____
Add Carry-over Points from Section 2			_____
Grand Total			_____
Subtract Points Redeemed			_____
Points to Be Carried Over			_____

Section Four

	Done Points	Bonus Points	Total
16. Be Quick to Be Slow	500	_____	_____
17. "But It's Not My Fault!"	500	_____	_____
18. Are Your Walls Strong?	500	_____	_____
19. Should Wise Guys Talk?	500	_____	_____
20. Taking the Shortcut	500	_____	_____
Add Puzzle Points			_____
Add Carry-over Points from Section 3			_____
Grand Total			_____
Subtract Points Redeemed			_____
Points to Be Carried Over			_____

Plant it Deep Review (50 points for each)

Prov. 8:17 _____
Neh. 8:10 _____
Gal. 6:9 _____
Prov. 27:17 _____
Prov. 11:9 _____
Prov. 14:30 _____
Prov. 16:3 _____
James 5:8 _____
Prov. 29:20 _____
Prov. 25:28 _____

Add Review Points _____
Add Carry-over Points from Section 4 _____
Grand Total _____
Points Redeemed _____

SECTION

1

THE Father WHO Loves

IT'S ALIVE!

I love those who love me, and those who seek me find me.

PROVERBS 8:17

LET'S DIG

1. Name six people you love:

- _____
- _____
- _____
- _____
- _____
- _____

2. How do these people know you love them?
3. When someone says they love you, how do you like them to show it?
4. When God told us he loved us, how did he show it?
5. How is he showing his love to you today?

Dad's turn

- When did you first realize that you really did love God?
- These days, how do you show God that you love him?
- How do you seek after God, and are you finding him? (Be honest!)

WHAT IF...

. . You lived in a family that said "I love you" all the time—but no one ever showed it. Everyone looked out for themselves and didn't bother making another family member's life a little better. Do verbal *I love you*s mean someone really loves you?

. . . You lived in a family who never said "I love you" to each other. They would do little things to show care and concern, but they *never* said those words. Do acts of care and concern mean someone really loves you?

NOW *What?*

God's love comes to us without any conditions. That is, there is nothing we can do to *earn* his love. But how does God know if we love him? By (a) the way we treat others and (b) how much we want to spend time with him.

According to the verse at the beginning, God wants us to love him and seek after him, correct? Write down three things you can do to *love* God this week:

- _____
- _____
- _____

Write down three things you can do to *seek* God this week:

- _____
- _____
- _____

OVERTIME CHALLENGE

(150 points)

- Proverbs 8:35. How can having God's favor help us in life?
- John 5:39-40. How does the Bible help us seek after God?
- Hebrews 10:22-23. What should we do to have a sincere heart?

PLANT IT DEEP

(150 points)

I love those who love me, and those who seek me find me. (Prov. 8:17)

Safe AND Secure

IT'S ALIVE!

He who fears the LORD has a secure fortress, and for his children it will be a refuge.

PROVERBS 14:26

LET'S DIG

1. Explain what your picture of a "secure fortress" looks like.
2. Do all of your friends believe in God or Jesus?
3. Why do some dads and families not believe?
4. Name six benefits of being a Christian:

- _____
- _____
- _____
- _____
- _____
- _____

5. Besides heaven, why would your dad want you to believe in Jesus?

Dad's turn

- Was there ever a time in your past when you felt insecure, like you didn't know what would happen from one day to the next? What did it feel like?
- What guarantees does this life hold?
- Why do you want your child to have the security of knowing God well enough to always run to him?

WHAT IF...

. . . You made arrangements with your mom to go over to a new friend's house to play after school. Walking the mile or so to their house was a blast. You joked and laughed and didn't even pay any attention to where you were going. After playing for a couple of hours, you noticed it was five-thirty—time to go home. You called your mom and told her you could find the way, no problem. She said, "Good, 'cause I've got stuff to do anyway."

As you started walking, you realized you'd never been on those streets before. You not only didn't know how to find your house, you also had no idea how to get back to your friend's house.

How would you feel, and what would you do?

. . . The same situation happened, but instead of being lost on unfamiliar roads, when you noticed you were lost, you recognized the street that led straight to your grandma's home!

How would you feel compared to the other situation?
Why do familiar people help you feel so much safer?

Now *What?*

Think of three situations that can be frightening if you don't know where you're going or where you are:

- _____
- _____
- _____

Life offers us a lot of situations that are new, unfamiliar, and sometimes even pretty scary. Though

Satan tries to keep Christians in the dark—wandering around by themselves—the passage at the beginning says that God is a strong fortress we can run to.

Your parents know that they can't be there your whole life to help you through every problem, but they know who can! Whatever new or uncertain situation occurs, God is always there to run to and to answer your plea for help. You can always feel safe when you realize he loves you enough to never leave you. That's why your folks work so hard to teach you about God. If he's a stranger to you, you're not going to want to run to him, right? But if you know him like the most trusted person in your life, you'll always be able to know what a fortress he really is.

In the three situations you wrote down, how can God bring security and peace?

OVERTIME CHALLENGE

(150 points)

- John 16:33. What are the two promises in this verse?
- Romans 8:37. How are we more than conquerors?
- 2 Corinthians 2:14. What's a "procession"? What kind of procession does God lead us in?

PRAY IT UP

Heavenly Father, first I want to thank you for my parents, who are trying to help me understand what you are really like. I know they love me and want only your best in my life. Second, I'd like to have a strong confidence in every situation I'm in. Help me to realize that no matter where I am, you're there to strengthen me, comfort me, guide me, and love me. I want to always have YOU to run to. Amen.

Where DO YOU FIND Happiness?

IT'S ALIVE!

A happy heart makes the face cheerful, but heartache crushes the spirit.

PROVERBS 15:13

LET'S DIG

1. Name six things (or people) that can make you happy:

- _____
- _____
- _____
- _____
- _____
- _____

2. Now, name six things (or people) that can make you sad (or make your heart ache):

- _____
- _____
- _____
- _____
- _____
- _____

3. Which list was easier to make? Why?
4. Do you think God promises we'll always be happy? (Hint: Try to recall one of the passages in chapter 2's "Overtime Challenge.")
5. Who is responsible for your happiness: you, your parents, or God?

20·15·10·5·0 BC

TIME SELECTOR

Dad's turn

- Were you a happy kid or someone who experienced a lot of heartache? Why?
- What's the difference between happiness, joy, and contentment? Which would you rather have?
- What are the things that make you happy and sad today?

WHAT IF...

. . You were able to choose those things that would make you happy each day, just like you would on a menu in a restaurant. Look at the "Happiness Menu" below. For each day of this make-believe week, choose two things that would make you happy. (You can use an item only twice.)

- Sunday:_____
- Monday:_____
- Tuesday:_____
- Wednesday:_____
- Thursday:_____
- Friday:_____
- Saturday:_____

HAPPINESS MENU

- a new bike
- listening to a tape with Dad
- a good grade on a test
- making a new friend
- baking cookies with Mom
- watching a TV show alone
- drawing a picture for Grandpa
- new shoes
- hearing about a relative who has become a Christian
- playing a board game with the family
- a new hat
- kicking the soccer ball with Dad
- playing Nintendo
- a field trip away from school
- a new baseball glove
- reading your Bible
- listening to music
- visiting sick children in the hospital
- listening to Grandma tell stories about Dad
- going for a hike with the family
- reading a book

Now *What?*

What you've just done is put a value on things you can do or *receive*. Next to each of the things you chose, write an *L* if the choice has long-term value (if it will make you happy or joyful for more than a day) or an *S* if it has short-term value.

Being happy about receiving things that only have short-term value isn't wrong, but if all of your selections have an *S*, it probably takes a lot of stuff to really make you happy. The key to real happiness would be having a good balance between the *L*'s and the *S*'s.

At the end of each day this week, you and Dad keep track of those things you do or receive that have "L-value" and "S-value." It will be fun to find out how balanced you are.

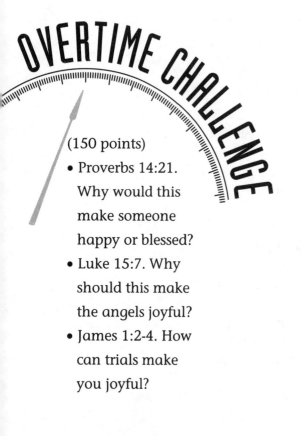

OVERTIME CHALLENGE

(150 points)

- Proverbs 14:21. Why would this make someone happy or blessed?
- Luke 15:7. Why should this make the angels joyful?
- James 1:2-4. How can trials make you joyful?

PLANT IT DEEP

(150 points)
Do not grieve, for the joy of the LORD is your strength. (Neh. 8:10)

4

A Good Choice

IT'S ALIVE!

Do not withhold good from those who deserve it, when it is in your power to act.

PROVERBS 3:27

LET'S DIG

1. Think of ten people you know who deserve to have something good happen to them.

- _____ • _____
- _____ • _____
- _____ • _____
- _____ • _____
- _____ • _____

2. Who has done something good for you at school, and what was it?

3. When was the last time you did something good for Mom? What was it?

4. Have you ever done something good for someone, but they didn't say thanks or do something good back to you? How did you feel?

5. Can you think of three reasons why we should think more about doing good things for others?

- _____
- _____
- _____

Dad's turn

- Think of a time when someone (other than your mom and dad) did something good for you during your younger years.
- Next, try to think of a time you did something good for someone else. What was their response?
- What are the top three reasons for doing something good for someone else?

- _____
- _____
- _____

WHAT IF...

. . The biggest bully in your class needed a pencil. He asked someone in front of you, but that person didn't have one.

Would you offer him one of your extras, or would you wait until he asked you?

. . . Someone you didn't know got hurt on the playground.

Would you offer to go to a teacher or school nurse and get a Band-Aid for them? Or would you think that someone else will probably help the person?

NOW *What?*

• Name one friend at school:_____.

What can you do that would help your friend in some way?

• Name someone at school you know but aren't necessarily friends with:_____.

What could you do to help this person in some way?

(150 points)
- Mark 9:41. How big does the good we do have to be?
- Galatians 6:9-10. Doing good may get tiring. Then what?
- Luke 18:19. Will good works get us to heaven?

PLANT IT DEEP

(150 points)

Let us not become weary in doing good, for at the proper time we will reap a harvest if we do not give up. (Gal. 6:9)

5

Master THE Motive

IT'S ALIVE!

All a man's ways seem innocent to him, but motives are weighed by the LORD.

PROVERBS 16:2

LET'S DIG

1. When was the last time you felt like you did something wrong?
2. Did you know it was wrong, or did you just know someone wouldn't be happy about what you did?
3. Is it good or bad to admit your mistakes?
4. What two mistakes are the hardest for you to admit?

- _____
- _____

5. What two mistakes are the easiest for you to admit?

- _____
- _____

Dad's turn

- What is a motive? What do good motives tell about a person? What do selfish motives tell about a person?
- When were you old enough to know whether you had good motives or selfish motives? How could you tell the difference?
- Why do you think God cares so much about what our motives are?

WHAT IF...

. . You were driving by a park in your town one summer morning with your dad, and you saw a young woman with two children asleep on one of the benches. After determining they really were homeless, you asked if you could stop by a store and buy them some food—you'll even use some of your own money!

Will these people ever be able to repay you? What do you think God thinks of this kind of motive?

. . . Your mom was doing some work around the house. When she asked if you could help, you asked, "How much will I get for it?" She said, "I thought you could help because you're a member of the family." You said, "But Mom, I need money to buy things."

What would your motives be? How could you have better motives?

NOW *What?*

Having pure motives *all* the time is nearly impossible. Our sinful and selfish nature is too strong. But that shouldn't prevent us from trying to take our eyes off of how everything can benefit us. Gaining extra money, more comfort, or our own way—especially at the expense of others—is a sad way to live life.

Try to think of one way Dad could help you have better motives without being a nag or making you feel guilty.

OVERTIME CHALLENGE

(150 points)

- Genesis 8:21. What does God know about our heart? Does that stop him from loving us?
- Proverbs 27:19. How do motives serve as a mirror of what's inside someone?
- 1 Corinthians 4:4-5. What will the Lord judge on the last day?

PRAY IT UP

Heavenly Father, you know very well that my motives for doing things—even good things—are not always the best. It's tough to realize that I'm not the most important person on this earth. But I really want my heart to become pure. I want my motives to be like yours. Help me to seek your forgiveness when they aren't, and help me to love and serve others more often—even when I know I'll receive nothing in return. Amen.

SECTION #1 BONUS PUZZLE
(1,000 Points)

....

```
R   A   S   S   U   R   A   N   C   E   P   W   Q   E
R   O   R   A   Z   E   T   I   F   E   N   E   B   I
E   P   Y   D   E   R   E   C   N   I   S   A   L   T
V   B   U   C   O   N   Q   U   E   R   O   R   S   E
E   C   O   C   X   S   T   R   A   E   H   Y   T   S
N   F   G   H   E   A   R   T   A   C   H   E   N   T
W   A   T   E   R   U   I   S   H   N   L   K   E   I
E   I   R   E   A   P   A   W   E   E   J   B   P   N
I   T   O   R   T   Y   L   P   M   V   E   J   E   G
G   H   U   F   E   S   S   O   F   A   V   O   R   O
H   F   B   U   H   W   J   E   X   E   I   Y   V   O
E   U   L   L   Q   U   A   D   E   H   T   F   C   D
D   L   E   C   A   E   P   R   A   K   O   U   L   A
B   T   N   E   G   I   L   I   D   I   M   L   T   B
```

<table>
<tr><td>ASSURANCE</td><td>HEARTACHE</td><td>SAD</td></tr>
<tr><td>BENEFIT</td><td>HEARTS</td><td>SEEK</td></tr>
<tr><td>CHEERFUL</td><td>HEAVEN</td><td>SINCERE</td></tr>
<tr><td>CONQUERORS</td><td>JOYFUL</td><td>TESTING</td></tr>
<tr><td>CUP</td><td>MOTIVE</td><td>TRIALS</td></tr>
<tr><td>DILIGENT</td><td>NEVER</td><td>TROUBLE</td></tr>
<tr><td>FAITHFUL</td><td>PEACE</td><td>WATER</td></tr>
<tr><td>FAVOR</td><td>REAP</td><td>WEARY</td></tr>
<tr><td>GOOD</td><td>REWARD</td><td>WEIGHED</td></tr>
</table>

SECTION

2

6

IS Every Pal A Friend?

IT'S ALIVE!

A righteous man is cautious in friendship, but the way of the wicked leads them astray.

PROVERBS 12:26

LET'S DIG

1. Name three qualities you look for in a good friend:

36

- _____
- _____
- _____

2. Name three things about yourself that others like about you:

- _____
- _____
- _____

3. Is choosing the right friends important? Why? Why not?
4. What can happen if you have the wrong friends?
5. How do you know whether to make someone a friend or to be cautious in the friendship?

20·15·10·5·0 BC
TIME SELECTOR

Dad's turn

- Describe one of your best friends when you were in grade school. Then talk about a friend you maybe shouldn't have had.
- Did your parents ever tell you not to be friends with someone? How did you respond? Why do you think they would do that?
- As you began to grow older, going into junior and senior high, what were the qualities you looked for in friends?

WHAT IF...

.. You had a friend that you did everything with. If you're a guy, you're shooting hoops, playing Nintendo, getting into water fights, walking up to the store—stuff like that. If you're a girl, you're fixing each other's hair, talking on the phone, shopping together, trying on each other's clothes—stuff like that.

The point is, you like to do stuff together! Things are going great until one day your friend starts spending time with someone else. When you call, your friend is always busy.

Write down some things either one of you may have done to ruin the friendship.

- _____
- _____
- _____
- _____

Why do friendships break up?

NOW *What?*

Choosing the right friends is one of the first and most important privileges parents usually give to their children. If their children choose wisely, that tells the parents they are not only growing up, they're maturing.

Maturity means more privileges, immaturity means less. Part of your "job" while you are growing up is making mistakes. How well you do in that job depends on whether you learn from them and then correct them!

Write down the five friends you are closest to. Then on a scale of one to ten (ten being best), rate these friends whether they're a good influence or a not-so-good influence on you.

NAME	RATING
1. _____	_____
2. _____	_____
3. _____	_____
4. _____	_____
5. _____	_____

Think about this: How would each of these people rate *you* as an influence on *them?*

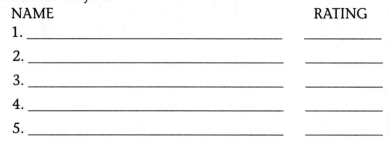

OVERTIME CHALLENGE

(150 points)
- Proverbs 22:24-25. Why shouldn't you make friends with a hot-tempered person?
- Proverbs 13:20. What happens if you walk with the wise?
- Proverbs 28:7. Why is a glutton so bad to be around?

PRAY IT UP

Dear Lord, you spent time with men who weren't perfect— even one who betrayed you. Yet you chose men who proved to be trustworthy, who were faithful to you, and who did their best. Help me to choose as wisely as you. But along with choosing good friends, help me to BE a good friend to everyone I'm with. Amen.

7

A Helping Hand

IT'S ALIVE!

Do not rebuke a mocker or he will hate you; rebuke a wise man and he will love you. Instruct a wise man and he will be wiser still; teach a righteous man and he will add to his learning.

PROVERBS 9:8-9

LET'S DIG

1. Have you ever told a friend they were doing something that might hurt them? What did they say in return?
2. Has anyone (besides your parents or a teacher) ever told you to change your behavior? How did you respond?
3. Should a friend tell you when you are messing up?
4. Under what circumstances would you want a friend to tell you to shape up? (What would you have to be doing?)
5. If a friend never confronts you when you are messing up, are they a very good friend?

Dad's turn

- Do you ever remember telling a friend to get his act together? What was it about?
- Did a friend ever confront you on your behavior?
- How have friends helped you in your relationship with God?

WHAT IF...

. . . A good friend was cheating on Friday math tests. Though he didn't cheat from your paper, you could see him look on a neighbor's paper as he sat two rows ahead of you. After nearly two months of seeing him cheat, you finally get up the nerve to say something to him while walking home from school.

What should you say to him? What shouldn't you say to him?

. . . Your Sunday school class took on the project of cleaning up a park across the street once a month. The whole class agreed to do it, but after the first time, you decided to skip it. When everyone asked where you were, you told them you had other plans and couldn't make it. One day after the class had cleaned the park, a good friend came by and saw you home watching TV. When he asked you why you didn't come, you said you didn't want to. As he pressed you on why you hadn't been there in the previous months, you told him you hadn't really been busy—you just didn't want to pick up other people's garbage.

What should he say that would help you see that what you were doing was wrong?

Pretend the person who came by wasn't a friend, just someone from class. Would they be able to say anything to help you be honest and to encourage you to come in the future?

NOW *What?*

As you grow older, friendships can take on a whole new level. Friends are more than just people you do stuff with—they are people you really care about.

When you care about someone, you are willing to say something occasionally to help them stay on the right path. You don't want them to get hurt or in trouble.

If you want to be a good friend to others, you don't have to be perfect yourself—you just have to care enough to help. Name six things you'd like to be able to say something about if your friend started doing them.

- _____
- _____
- _____

- _____
- _____
- _____

The next time a friend does one of these, ask your dad how you can best help them.

OVERTIME CHALLENGE

(150 points)
- Proverbs 17:17. How does adversity bring you close to a friend?
- Proverbs 18:24. How can a close friend be better than many acquaintances?
- Proverbs 27:6. Why are wounds from a friend trustworthy?

PLANT IT DEEP

(150 points)
As iron sharpens iron, so one man sharpens another. (Prov. 27:17)

8

Who MADE THE Target?

IT'S ALIVE!

He who mocks the poor shows contempt for their Maker; whoever gloats over disaster will not go unpunished.

PROVERBS 17:5

LET'S DIG

1. Do kids make fun of others at school?
2. Who gets made fun of the most? (Either name an individual or a type of person.)
3. If someone gets made fun of all the time, how do you think it makes that person feel?
4. When, or under what circumstances, are you most tempted to make fun of another person? school? church? neighborhood? home?
5. Does anyone ever try to stick up for those kids who are made fun of?

Dad's turn

- Recall a few kids who were made fun of when you were in school. Why were they made fun of? Did you ever join in?
- When did you realize that everyone was made by God and deserved to be treated as a special creation? How did that change the way you treated others?
- Tell your child what you hope he or she will do around those who are made fun of.

WHAT IF...

. . . When you arrived at school one day, four or five kids began to tease you about what you were wearing. They kept it up through recess, lunch, and then even after school. The next day you arrived at school wearing what everyone else wears, and those kids had so much fun the day before, they found something else to make fun of. You began to wonder if this was going to be a daily habit of theirs.

How would you feel?

What would you do to try to stop them?

How would you feel if none of your friends tried to do anything to stop them for fear that they would be the target instead?

. . . There was a girl at school who wore glasses, was more than a little overweight, and didn't dress very well. Boys *and* girls at school made fun of her because she was so—different and not very attractive.

What has she actually done to be treated so poorly?

What does God think of her?

What would happen to you if you told your friends to stop teasing her? Would you be able to survive that?

Now *What?*

When people make fun of others for reasons like looks, skin color, clothes, lack of athletic ability, weight, height, etc., four things could be happening:

1. They're not very secure themselves, so they have to draw attention away from their own flaws to make sure they're not noticed;

2. they are trying to tear someone else down to make themselves look better by comparison;

3. they really don't believe God made and loves that person; or

4. they are developing a habit of "selective love" that is really a bad character quality to have.

Making fun of others, unfortunately, is a fact of life as you go through grade school and up. But that doesn't mean you have to participate in it. And you should try to discourage others from doing it. People need to realize how destructive it can be.

This week, try not to make fun of anyone else. Try to look at people the way God does.

OVERTIME CHALLENGE

(150 points)

- Proverbs 11:9. What is used to destroy someone? What can help us escape?

- Proverbs 4:24. How is making fun of others "perverse"?

- Proverbs 14:31. What do you do when you "oppress" someone?

PLANT IT DEEP

(150 points)
With his mouth the godless destroys his neighbor, but through knowledge the righteous escape.
(Prov. 11:9)

9

GIVING
Courage

IT'S ALIVE!

An anxious heart weighs a man down, but a kind word cheers him up.

PROVERBS 12:25

LET'S DIG

1. What two things do you get most anxious about?

   - _____
   - _____

2. What usually helps to keep you from being too anxious?
3. How do you feel when others encourage you?
4. Do you ever encourage others? How?
5. How do you feel after you encourage someone who is down or nervous?

Dad's turn

- When you were in school, what made you most nervous or anxious?
- Who encouraged you most? What did they say? Did you like to be friends with others who were encouragers?
- Is it fun to be an encourager? How can someone become a better encourager?

WHAT IF...

... A friend's parents were considering getting a divorce. Most of each school day he was nervous, not knowing if his dad was going to come home that night or not.
What could you do to encourage him?

... Your older brother was studying for a big test he had to take. He'd spent two weeks studying, and the test was only two days away.
What could you do to encourage him?

... You heard that the place where your dad works was seriously considering shutting down. That would mean he would have to find work real fast. You could tell he was nervous.
What could you do to encourage him?

NOW *What?*

You can't control the times when you need encouragement from others. They have to see how anxious you are and try to help on their own. But you can control how much courage *you give* to others. People who are encouragers usually have a lot of friends, are fun to be around, and usually are encouraged a lot themselves.

Think of two people who need encouragement. Write down the names of those two people next to the numbers. Below their names, write down three ways you can encourage them in the next three days.

1.

• _____

• _____

• _____

2.

- _____
- _____
- _____

OVERTIME CHALLENGE

(150 points)
- Proverbs 15:30. What two things can help someone?
- Proverbs 15:23. What are the benefits of encouraging others?
- Proverbs 25:11. Are the words we speak to others important?

PRAY IT UP

Dear Lord, you are well aware of the times that I need to be encouraged. During those times, please bring someone my way who will give me that courage. But more than that, I want to be used by you to give others courage. Help me to look for times to say the right thing or give someone a smile when they're down—not just this week, but for the rest of my life. Amen

10

It Rots THE Bones

IT'S ALIVE!

A heart at peace gives life to the body, but envy rots the bones.

PROVERBS 14:30

LET'S DIG

1. Envy is resenting an advantage someone has over you and then wanting that same advantage for yourself. What would someone envy about you?

2. Think of the popular kids at church or school. Do you envy anything about them?

3. Name four good things you can envy about other people:

   - _____
   - _____
   - _____
   - _____

4. Name four not-so-good things you can envy about other people:

   - _____
   - _____
   - _____
   - _____

Dad's turn

- Were you more likely to envy brothers and sisters or friends from school?
- What types of things did you envy about them? What did envying others ever give you?
- What do you think is the reason envy can be so destructive?

WHAT IF...

. . . One of your friends told you a story about how their family helped out one Saturday in a local homeless shelter. She talked about giving some toys to other kids her age, serving coffee and other food, and spending four hours doing odds and ends for the pastor and his wife who ran the facility. What might you "envy" about that?

. . . One of your friends was just a natural at sports. No matter what they tried out for, or what they did in PE, they were the best. And because they were so good at everything, they were liked by nearly everyone at school.
   What is it about this person that could be envied?
   Can that person help it if people envy their talents?

NOW *What?*

Envy is not always as bad as jealousy. In fact, there are good things we can be envious of: character qualities that remind us of Jesus, the ability to talk to people without getting nervous, good works, a knowledge of Scripture, etc.

   Think of *one good thing* that you can be envious of, and start pursuing it. You can do that by reading up on it if it's something to know, practicing it if it's a skill or character quality, and being more disciplined if it's something you want to work on.

OVERTIME CHALLENGE

(150 points)

- Proverbs 3:31. Why shouldn't we envy this type of person?
- 1 Corinthians 13:4. Is this a positive or a negative type of envy?
- James 3:14-16. What can happen if envy is allowed to take hold of a person?

PLANT IT DEEP

(150 points)

A heart at peace gives life to the body, but envy rots the bones. (Prov. 14:30)

BONUS PUZZLE #2

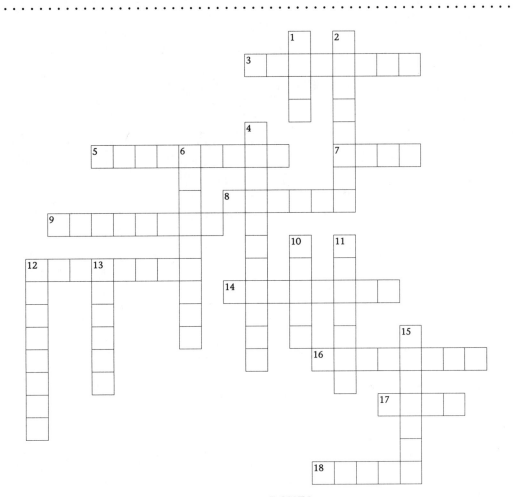

ACROSS

3 "___ are the wounds of a friend" (Prov. 27:6)
5 "A ___ of fools suffers harm" (Prov. 13:20)
7 "Love is patient and kind. Love doesn't ___"
   (1 Cor. 13:4)
8 "There is a friend who ___ closer than a
   brother" (Prov. 18:24)
9 If you make friends with a hot- tempered
   man, you could become ___ (Prov. 22:25)
12 "A righteous man is ___ in friendships"
   (Prov. 12:26)
14 A godless man's mouth ___ his neighbor
   (Prov. 11:9)
16 "An ___ heart weighs it down" (Prov. 12:25)
17 "Love doesn't envy or boast and is not ___"
   (1 Cor. 13:4)
18 "Love doesn't envy or ___" (1 Cor. 13:4)

DOWN

1 "Love is patient and ___ " (1 Cor. 13:4)
2 "As iron ___ iron, so one man does another"
   (Prov. 27:17)
4 "Don't make friends with a ___-___ man"
   (Prov. 22:24)
6 "A brother is born for ___" (Prov. 17:7)
10 "A word ___ spoken is like apples of gold in
   a setting of silver" (Prov. 25:11)
11 "Do not envy a ___ man" (Prov. 3:31)
12 "He who mocks the poor shows ___ for their
   maker" (Prov. 17:5)
13 "How good is a ___ word" (Prov. 15:23)
15 "Keep ___ talk from your lips" (Prov. 4:24)

You Give, He Takes, EVERYONE Wins!

IT'S ALIVE!

Commit to the LORD whatever you do, and your plans will succeed.

PROVERBS 16:3

LET'S DIG

1. When you make a commitment, what does that mean you'll do?
2. Have you ever broken a commitment? What was it?
3. Could you have fulfilled that commitment? How?
4. Name three things you would like to succeed in:

- _____
- _____
- _____

5. Pick one, and write down all that you think is needed to be successful:

Dad's turn

- What were some of the earliest commitments you made when you were a kid? Did you stick with all of them?
- How do you commit something to the Lord?
- Talk about a few things that you have committed to the Lord and what the result has been.

WHAT IF...

. . You had a neighbor friend whose family didn't attend church. Since this was one of your best friends, you wanted to do what you could to make sure this friend knew about Jesus and had the opportunity to accept him and go to heaven.

You knew that doing something as significant as this wouldn't be easy. Your plan was to find events at church they would like to go to and then invite them.

With your dad's help, list some other things you can do, and discuss how you could "commit" this to the Lord.

NOW *What?*

Though this may seem like one of those lessons you'll need more "in the future," you'd be surprised at all of the things that come up in your life that you need to commit to God. Committing something to him (a plan, a game, an assignment, etc.) means taking the results out of your hands and putting them into God's. It makes *him* responsible for what happens! What's your responsibility?

1. To always try your best

2. To persevere when the going gets tough ('cause it will!)

3. To try not to "own" the results yourself, always believing you'd rather have God's best—no matter what it is—than your best

Choose a real-life event in your world that needs not only your best but God's results. How can you commit this to *him* without taking it back?

OVERTIME CHALLENGE

(150 points)
- Luke 23:46. How did this commitment help Jesus?
- Psalm 37:4-5. How can you "delight yourself in the Lord"?
- Psalm 57:2. What is God's promise to your request?

PLANT IT DEEP

(150 points)
Commit to the LORD whatever you do, and your plans will succeed. (Prov. 16:3)

12

TO **Work** OR NOT TO **Work?**

IT'S ALIVE!

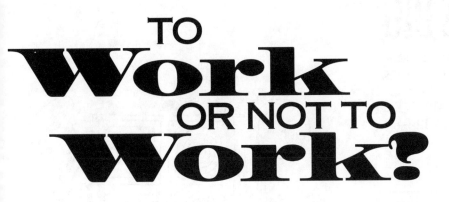

He who works his land will have abundant food, but he who chases fantasies lacks judgment.

PROVERBS 12:11

LET'S DIG

1. Effort usually equals reward. Besides work, think of two other things you can do where effort equals reward:

• _____

• _____

2. What do you think "chasing fantasies" means?
3. What's the difference between bad judgment and good judgment? How do you get good judgment?
4. What reward would you have if your dad or mom didn't work?
5. Do you think it's important that you learn the value of work?

Dad's turn

• Did you have to do chores when you were growing up? What were the rewards? What did you learn?
• Were there ever times when you just didn't want to work? Were you ever rewarded for those times?
• What are your thoughts on work as an adult? What do you do now during those times when you don't feel like working?

WHAT IF...

. . You had a test tomorrow in school. The problem was that one of your favorite hours of TV was on tonight. Your parents give you the choice as to what you should do.

What will you do? What are the rewards or consequences for your choice?

. . . In order to receive your allowance, you had to help Mom around the house and keep your room clean. For a couple of weeks in a row, your room just couldn't seem to stay clean, and you didn't make time to help around the house.

Should you get your allowance anyway?

Now *What?*

When you're growing up, you're allowed a pretty large amount of time to goof around ("chase fantasies"). You're not old enough to make enough money for a family to live on, and you need to play to help you grow. But your grade-school years are also the time to start learning how valuable it is to work—and that work can give you rewards. However, not every task you do beyond the ordinary needs to have a reward. Sometimes just contributing to the family is reward enough.

Write down four things you can do, either around the house or for others, that don't need to be rewarded.

- _____   • _____
- _____   • _____

This week, pick one you can do, do it, and don't tell anyone else what you're doing. Then tell Dad next week what it was and how you felt after it was over.

OVERTIME CHALLENGE

(200 points)

- Proverbs 14:23. What's the difference between hard work and talk?
- 2 Thessalonians 3:6-13. What lessons do you see in this passage?
- Titus 3:14. What does this say about rewards?

PRAY IT UP

Dear heavenly Father, I thank you for the rewards I receive from others who work: my dad and mom who work so hard to pay bills and keep the house in order. I know that sometimes they'd rather be doing other things besides helping to make my life as good as it is. Though I'm young, I realize how important it is to work, not just for rewards I can see, but for the sake of helping. Help me to see that as a reward as well. Help me to learn the value of work. Amen.

13

Every
Dad's
Nightmare

IT'S ALIVE!

Lazy hands make a man poor, but diligent hands bring wealth.

PROVERBS 10:4

LET'S DIG

1. What are the times when it's fun to be lazy?
2. Would you like to be lazy all the time?
3. Where do you think that would lead?
4. What do you think it means to be "diligent"? (Dad, you can help.)
5. When are you most likely to be rewarded: when you're lazy or when you're diligent? Why?

Dad's turn

- Did anyone ever consider you a lazy person? In what areas?
- What did you learn that helped you overcome laziness in those areas?
- How would you feel about having a child who was lazy in a lot of ways and diligent in only a few?

WHAT IF...

. . Your coach told you that to be good in basketball, you needed to shoot for one hour and dribble for thirty minutes a day. Since you really wanted to be a top player, for two weeks you did exactly as he asked. But finally, you got tired of being diligent and decided you wanted to read or watch TV instead.

Will you reach your goal of being a top player?

How is *hoping* to reach a goal different from *working* toward it?

. . . Your teacher said that if you read the first two chapters out of your social studies textbook, you would do well on the Friday test. Instead of reading them, however, you skimmed through the major headings and didn't read the text word for word.

How well will you be rewarded for your work?

Why is it so tempting to slack off when it comes to schoolwork?

NOW *What?*

Everyone likes to be lazy at times. Relaxing is good for us. But some kids (and parents) are practically addicted to laziness. Pick one area below that you are most tempted to be lazy in, and develop a strategy with Dad that will help you overcome the habit of laziness.

Possible choices:

1. Schoolwork 2. Chores 3. Music practice
4. Prayer 5. Athletic practice 6. Reading for enjoyment 7. Other:_____

Area chosen: _____

Roadblocks to diligence:
1. TV   2. Friends   3. No immediate rewards
4. Video games   5. The radio or tape deck
6. Talking on the phone   7. Being tired
8. Other:_____

Ways Dad can help: Without nagging, how can Dad—or Mom—help you overcome laziness in this area?

- _____   - _____
- _____   - _____

This week's strategy: small things you can do to help you reach your goal

- _____   - _____
- _____   - _____

OVERTIME CHALLENGE

(150 points)
- Proverbs 13:4. What are the rewards of the diligent?
- Proverbs 21:5. What is a characteristic of the diligent?
- Proverbs 26:13. What does this verse tell us about a lazy person?

PRAY IT UP

Dear heavenly Father, I know what you have to say about laziness. And I also know the consequences for not being diligent. I don't want to be lazy because I realize that in the long run it will hurt me. Help me, Lord, to overcome in this one area. I need your strength to do it. Remind Dad to help me, and teach me to be a more diligent person who doesn't make a habit of being lazy. Amen.

14

TO BE
Patient,
OR NOT TO BE,
THAT IS THE
Question

71

IT'S ALIVE!

*A patient man has great under-
standing, but a quick-tempered
man displays folly.*

PROVERBS 14:29

LET'S DIG

1. What is tough for you to be patient in?
2. We get impatient when we don't get our way or if something we want to happen isn't happening in a short amount of time. Is that true for you?
3. Have you ever faced any consequences for your impatience? What were they?
4. How can you tell when you are getting impatient?
5. Does anything good ever happen when you are quick-tempered instead of patient?

20·15·10·5·0 BC

TIME SELECTOR

Dad's turn

- When you were growing up, what used to cause you to lose your patience?
- What makes you impatient today?
- What types of consequences do you (did you) face for your impatience?

WHAT IF...

. . . Someone from your class was always bugging you. They would take your pencil, smash your lunch interrupt when you tried to talk to someone —they were just plain annoying!

How long could you be patient with such a person?

What would you do when you finally lost your patience?

What should you do?

. . . You were in a soccer game, and the other team was playing pretty rough. Whenever you were dribbling the ball upfield, they were pushing and shoving. Not only were you getting ticked at your opponents, but also at the referee who wasn't calling any of the rough stuff! After getting knocked down for the third time with no call, you felt like you just had to say something.

What would you say?

How would you say it?

What would that accomplish?

NOW *What?*

If we're honest, we have to admit that sometimes exploding in anger, saying something hurtful to someone we're impatient with, feels *good!* That's why we do it. It temporarily allows us to get back at another person who is causing us frustration. Very rarely, however, does exploding impatience (anger) satisfy for longer than a few seconds. Why? Because it's not right.

When we're impatient, it's because we're *not getting what we want when we want it.* Welcome to life. Ask anyone over the age of twenty, and they'll tell you that's what life offers. So the key is learning how to *respond* appropriately when we're frustrated, rather than just *reacting* out of our feelings.

See if you can describe an emotional *reaction* and a more appropriate *response* to each of the "What If" situations above.

God wants to develop within us the character quality of patience. It's important to him because it's one of *his* qualities with *us*. He is always patient—even when we make the same mistake over and over. He doesn't get frustrated or lose his temper either.

Do you want to be a patient person? If you do, that means you want to be more like Jesus.

74

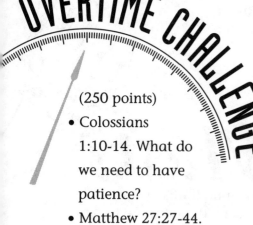

OVERTIME CHALLENGE

(250 points)

- Colossians 1:10-14. What do we need to have patience?
- Matthew 27:27-44. Why didn't Jesus *react* to his accusers?
- 2 Peter 3:8-9. Why is God patient with people?

PLANT IT DEEP

(150 points)
You too, be patient and stand firm, because the Lord's coming is near. (James 5:8)

15

ARE YOU
Vinegar
Smoke?

IT'S ALIVE!

As vinegar to the teeth and smoke to the eyes, so is a sluggard to those who send him.

PROVERBS 10:26

LET'S DIG

1. Have you ever tasted vinegar or had smoke in your eyes? How does it feel?
2. When you've been asked to do something important for someone, how do you feel? Do you want to come through or let them down?
3. Should you be trusted in little things or big things first? Why?
4. Do you sometimes wish your parents would trust you more?
5. To prove that you are a faithful person, what should you do?

Dad's Turn

- Was being faithful and trusted by others important to you when you were a kid? Why or why not?
- Tell about a time when you trusted someone to come through for you, but they let you down. How did you feel? Did you want to trust that person again?
- Does God think you're trustworthy? What has he entrusted you with?

76

WHAT IF...

... Two of your chores each day were to pick up your room and make your bed. For doing that you got one dollar a week as an allowance. You managed to accomplish that task about four days a week. You thought you were doing well, so you decided a good plan would be to ask your parents if you could do more chores for a larger allowance.

Have you been faithful in the tasks they've asked you to do?

Should you be trusted with more responsibility and a larger allowance?

NOW *What?*

For the rest of your life, you'll be asked to be faithful in small things before being given bigger responsibilities (and often bigger rewards).

• Teachers won't trust you with seventh-grade math until you conquer sixth-grade math.

• A driver's license won't appear in your wallet until you take driver's education in high school—and you do A LOT of practicing with Mom or Dad.

• You can't be manager at McDonald's until you flip burgers for a while.

The proverb above talks about being a messenger, but the real lesson is faithfulness—can you be trusted?

Think of one privilege you would like to have or goal you would like to shoot for. With your dad's help, try to write down the steps necessary to attain that privilege or goal.

OVERTIME CHALLENGE

(200 points)

- Luke 19:11-27. What is the main point of this story?
- 1 Timothy 1:12-16. Paul wanted to be faithful in what area?
- Proverbs 20:6. Who are the faithful people in your life?

PRAY IT UP

Dear heavenly Father, you have been faithful to me and my family for a long time. You are always trustworthy because you've always done what you say. Help me to first be faithful to you. Remind me to be faithful to you when I allow other things to come into my life that temporarily push you aside. And then help me to learn how not to be "vinegar smoke." I want to be faithful in small things so that I can be trusted with bigger things. Amen.

SECTION #3 BONUS PUZZLE
(1,000 Points)

....

```
W  E  M  U  P  P  U  R  P  O  S  E  A
D  T  R  B  U  S  Y  B  O  D  I  E  S
F  O  I  Y  L  L  O  F  V  S  H  J  M
T  I  F  O  R  P  Z  R  E  U  C  U  R
N  L  C  H  A  S  E  S  R  C  O  M  A
D  I  L  I  G  E  N  T  T  C  M  I  G
C  N  B  Q  U  A  H  L  Y  E  M  N  E
A  G  N  I  R  O  B  A  L  E  I  A  N
G  F  A  I  T  H  F  U  L  D  T  S  I
B  D  E  B  M  Y  K  P  N  E  P  U  V
U  E  S  L  U  G  G  A  R  D  L  W  C
L  T  A  M  B  F  T  T  E  A  D  J
A  S  L  N  O  S  V  I  R  L  E  N  I
E  U  R  A  R  K  W  E  O  I  T  K  T
C  R  I  E  Z  U  E  N  F  G  S  B  C
L  T  D  C  X  Y  W  T  F  H  A  B  A
D  N  O  P  S  E  R  J  E  T  H  L  E
U  R  I  S  A  T  I  S  F  I  E  D  R
```

79

ABUNDANT	HASTE	RESPOND
BUSYBODIES	IDLE	SATISFIED
CHASES	LABORING	SLUGGARD
COMMIT	LAZY	SMOKE
DELIGHT	MINAS	SUCCEED
DILIGENT	PATIENT	TOILING
EFFORT	POVERTY	TRUSTED
FAITHFUL	PROFIT	UNDERSTANDING
FIRM	PURPOSE	VINEGAR
FOLLY	REACT	

SECTION

4

16

BE Quick TO BE Slow

IT'S ALIVE!

It is not good to have zeal without knowledge, nor to be hasty and miss the way.

PROVERBS 19:2

LET'S DIG

1. What do you get most excited about?
2. Can you think of a time when you jumped into something too soon and should have waited?
3. With your dad, come up with a good example of having "zeal without knowledge."
4. Do you have a tendency to:
   ___ speak too quickly
   ___ spend too quickly
   ___ judge others too quickly
   ___ jump into fun things too quickly
5. Why do you think learning how to wait is important?

Dad's turn

- Were you ever known as someone who spoke or did things before you thought about what you should say or do?
- Can you remember a time when speaking too quickly got you in trouble?
- How have you learned not to be hasty in making decisions? spending money? speaking? judging others?

WHAT IF...

. . . Your friends all jumped off a cliff. Would you follow? (I had to ask that one because when I was a teenager, my mom always asked me that. It's probably a line you'll hear from your parents a lot as you continue to grow up. Give them a break—they mean well! P.S. The answer is no.)

. . . A new kid arrived at school about a month after school started. You already had a group of friends that you hung around with, but you knew this new person probably would feel less fearful and more comfortable if someone took the chance and tried to befriend them.

At recess, you went up and invited the new kid to get in on the foursquare game. The reply: "No, I don't like foursquare."

What would you be thinking about that person?

Are they saying, "I don't want to be your friend; get lost"? Or could their remark mean something else?

Would you try to start another conversation with them?

NOW *What?*

It's easy to act quickly. Thinking before you speak, spend, judge, or do fun things takes practice. Most people would say it just takes making foolish mistakes before you finally learn to be less hasty. While there are several areas we need to think through before jumping in with both feet (or with our tongue or cash), there are some things we don't need to think on too long.

With your dad, think of ten things you can be quick to do or say that would help you or other people:

- _____
- _____
- _____
- _____
- _____

- _____
- _____
- _____
- _____
- _____

This week, try to do all ten. (Give yourself 25 points for each one you can do.)

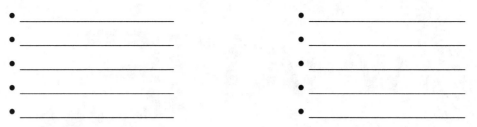

OVERTIME CHALLENGE

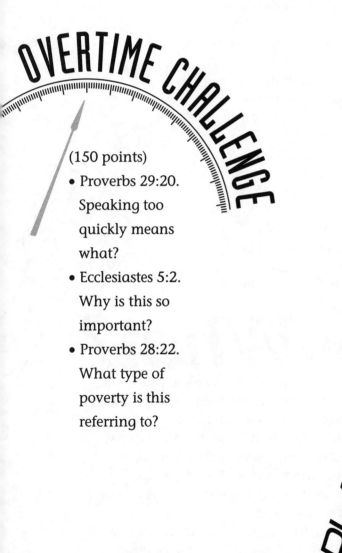

(150 points)
- Proverbs 29:20. Speaking too quickly means what?
- Ecclesiastes 5:2. Why is this so important?
- Proverbs 28:22. What type of poverty is this referring to?

PLANT IT DEEP

(150 points)
Do you see a man who speaks in haste? There is more hope for a fool than for him. (Prov. 29:20)

17

"But IT'S Not My Fault?"

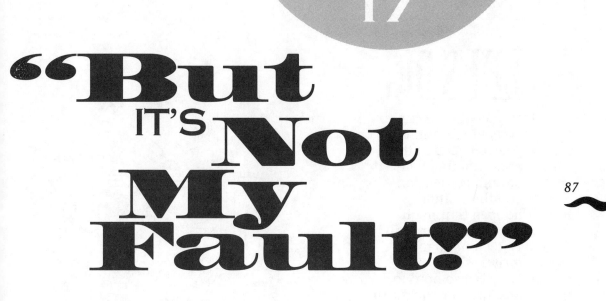

IT'S ALIVE!

A man's own folly ruins his life, yet his heart rages against the LORD.

PROVERBS 19:3

LET'S DIG

1. What does it mean to accept responsibility?
2. Are you good at this, or do you find yourself blaming others for bad things that happen that might have been your fault?
3. Is it wrong to make mistakes?
4. Why is it so hard to face the consequences for our mistakes?
5. Have you ever blamed God for something that happened?

Dad's turn

- When you were a kid, were you more likely to get in trouble for doing something wrong or for not taking responsibility for your actions?
- Why do you think God gets the blame for so many things? Have you ever blamed God for something that really wasn't his fault?
- What does it tell about a person if they are willing and able to accept responsibility? How about if they're not?

WHAT IF...

. . . You were at a friend's birthday party on a Saturday afternoon. After cake and presents, the dad told everyone to go outside for some games he had planned. As everyone was heading outside, you and another kid stopped to look at a cool present your friend got. You picked it up to look it over, and the other person said, "Let me see it." You handed it to him but let go of it before he grabbed it. It fell to the hard, linoleum floor and broke. No one was around besides the two of you. You looked at each other, then headed outside without saying a word.

Later, when everyone came back inside, the birthday boy noticed his present was broken. He asked what happened.

What do you honestly think you would do?

What do you think the consequences would be, if any, if you took responsibility for the broken toy?

. . . School was out and your family was about ready to go on the biggest and best vacation ever (pick a place you'd really like to go to). As a family you'd been planning this vacation for months. You were even crossing the days off on your calendar!

Two days before you were supposed to go, your mom accidentally tripped over something and hurt her leg really bad. She couldn't move it. You called your dad at work, and he rushed right home. He called 911, and the ambulance came to take her to the hospital. The doctors told you that she broke her leg in three places, she'll be in bed for two weeks, and she will have to wear a walking cast for two months. Vacation canceled.

How do you feel? Do you feel like blaming someone? Are you tempted to blame God for this?

NOW *What?*

As you get older, you'll notice that people with poor character rarely take responsibility for their own actions. They can't face the fact that they made a mistake, so they blame others.

Becoming a mature Christian means developing the ability to recognize and admit when you've messed up—no matter what the consequences could be.

One way to get started is to take responsibility for anything you've done in the past that you haven't already admitted. Starting fresh with a clean slate and building the habit of taking responsibility is very important. With that in mind, is there anything you need to tell your dad about? Now would be a good time!

OVERTIME CHALLENGE

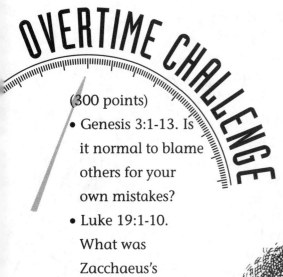

(300 points)

• Genesis 3:1-13. Is it normal to blame others for your own mistakes?

• Luke 19:1-10. What was Zacchaeus's reward for taking responsibility?

• Acts 5:1-11. What were the consequences for not taking responsibility?

PRAY IT UP

Dear Lord, taking responsibility for stuff I've done wrong is hard to do. I know you know that. But I want to be a person who isn't afraid to admit my mistakes—to YOU or others. Though it won't always feel good to admit when I'm wrong, give me the strength to do it. I don't want to be like those who always blame others for their problems. I want to be a person of character. Amen.

18

ARE YOUR Walls Strong?

IT'S ALIVE!

Like a city whose walls are broken down is a man who lacks self-control.

PROVERBS 25:28

LET'S DIG

1. What would likely happen to a city whose walls were broken down?
2. Would the inhabitants feel safe?
3. What is self-control? (Think of an example.)
4. How does having self-control make someone feel strong?
5. Name six things you've noticed that people have a tough time having self-control in:

- _____
- _____
- _____
- _____
- _____
- _____

Dad's turn

- When you were in grade school, what were the toughest areas for you to have self-control in?
- When did you finally learn that having self-control was important? Did that change you in any way?
- Can you think of people you know who don't have self-control in an area of their life? What have been the consequences for them?

WHAT IF...

... Your dad *gave* you a twenty-dollar bill so you could buy your mom a birthday present. He took you to Target and told you to go find something she'd like. But instead of looking in the mom-type sections, you went to the toy section. Naturally, you found something you *really* wanted.

You have three choices:

1. Buy the item you want, and say you're sorry later;
2. find something you want to buy, but save a little to buy Mom something too; or
3. spend the money on Mom.

What are you (really) leaning toward doing?

... Your mom and dad were going out on a date, so they got a baby-sitter to watch you. They told you (not the baby-sitter) you could only play one hour of Nintendo (or watch two hours of TV, whichever you wanted). You agreed.

Since the baby-sitter doesn't know the agreement, it would be easy to do both or to do one of them longer than the agreement.

How strong are the walls of your city? (What will you do?)

NOW *What?*

Self-control is something we humans always struggle with. Whether it's eating, watching TV, playing games, spending money—whatever—we are often tempted to go overboard. But *being tempted* to go overboard and actually *going* overboard are two different things. Answer these questions.

What are the consequences if you can't control your eating?

What are the consequences if you can't control your spending?

What are the consequences if you can't control your TV or entertainment habits?

See what can happen without self-control? Satan moves in and keeps your life from being as good as it could have been. For some people, going overboard in a certain area has become a habit they can't break! But the Holy Spirit is available to help us develop self-control and to remind us when we're losing it.

Write down the one area in your life that can use some self-control. Together with Dad, think of a strategy to get it under control . . . before it controls you.

94

OVERTIME CHALLENGE

(225 points)
- 2 Peter 1:5-8. What is the progression toward self-control, and where does it lead? (Make a circle diagram if it helps.)
- 2 Timothy 3:1-5. Which of these characteristics sticks out to you?
- Galatians 5:22-23. How can you get self-control?

PLANT IT DEEP

(150 points)
Like a city whose walls are broken down is a man who lacks self-control. (Prov. 25:28)

19

SHOULD Wise Guys Talk?

IT'S ALIVE!

Do you see a man wise in his own eyes? There is more hope for a fool than for him.

PROVERBS 26:12

LET'S DIG

1. Name four things you are good at:

- _____
- _____
- _____
- _____

2. Do you think it's OK to feel good about yourself for the things you are good at?
3. What about telling others you are good at something—is that a good idea?
4. How do you feel about other kids who talk about how good they are in something?
5. Why do you think people do that?

Dad's turn

- What were you pretty good at when you were a kid? Did others tell you you were good at it, or did you have to "remind" them?
- Do you know people now who think—and act—like they know it all? Do you like to be around those people?
- What's the difference between being *confident* in your ability and *bragging* about what you can do?

WHAT IF...

. . . You got straight A's in school. What two ways would you want to be rewarded? (Choose from the list below.)

. . . Without being asked, you helped your parents clean the whole house on a Saturday when you could have been playing with a friend. What two ways would you want to be rewarded?

. . . You made the game-winning basket for your team in an important game. What two ways would you want to be rewarded?

. . . You went with your dad to a local children's hospital and made friends with a kid who had cancer. What two ways would you want to be rewarded?

a. Parents or relatives give you money
b. Your friends let you know they appreciate that quality about you
c. Know that God was happy about it
d. Have Mom and Dad sit down, look you in the eye, and let you know how proud they are of you
e. Get an award at a school assembly
f. Tell others about what you did
g. Have your allowance raised
h. The feeling you got for doing it
i. Have your parents' friends come up to you and tell you "good job"
j. You get a special card telling you thanks

NOW *What?*

Did you see any patterns develop on the type of reward you thought would be best? If so, are they good patterns?

All of us like it when others give us attention or rewards for things that we do. It's fun to be noticed in a good way! But it's *really* fun when we wait until others do the noticing. And it's *really, really* fun to realize that God notices too. As you grow older, pleasing God, not getting rewards, is what really feels good.

This passage talks about being considered a fool when you look at yourself too highly. What two things do you do for an immediate reward?

• _____   • _____

Are there other rewards that you can wait for that would be better?

OVERTIME CHALLENGE

(150 points)

• Proverbs 27:2. Who should be the talker?

• Romans 12:16. What is one way not to get more proud of yourself than you should?

• Proverbs 3:7. What is evil about being wise in your own eyes?

PRAY IT UP

Dear heavenly Father, it's tempting to want to take the credit for things that I do. Even though it's not bad to feel good about what I can accomplish, help me to realize that the mind I have, the skills I have, and the good things I do are all because you've allowed me to do them. Help me to do things that are pleasing to you. Amen.

20

Taking
THE
Shortcut

IT'S ALIVE!

Trust in the LORD with all your heart and lean not on your own understanding; in all your ways acknowledge him, and he will make your paths straight.

PROVERBS 3:5-6

LET'S DIG

1. What is your definition of trust?
2. Who or what do you most rely on when you're in trouble? Why?
3. Why is it not a good idea to lean on your own understanding?
4. What's the difference between a straight path and a crooked one when you're walking toward a goal?
5. Do you sometimes forget how important it is to acknowledge God and trust in him day by day?

Dad's turn

- Many men learn at a young age not to trust anyone but themselves. Was that true with you? What did that attitude ever get you?
- What helped you to realize that trusting God was the way to go? How did that change you?
- What are ways you acknowledge God on a day by day basis? Do you sometimes forget to do that?

WHAT IF...

. . . You wanted to learn more about working with wood and building things. Who would you trust to teach you?

. . . You wanted to know how to shop for clothes so you could get the best bargains. Who would you trust to show you how?

. . . You wanted to be an awesome tennis player. Who would you trust to teach you?

. . . You wanted to be able to swim for long distances. Who would you trust to teach you?

. . . You wanted to know how to best go through life. Who is the most trustworthy to show you how?

NOW *What?*

The last "What If" has one answer: God. But many people don't see it that way. In fact, most rely on only one person to see them through life: themselves. That's why there is so much crime, drugs, homelessness, and broken relationships. People wanted to do it their own way, so now they're paying the consequences.

The challenge to trust God in everything is an invitation, not a command. God doesn't force us to lean on him. He lovingly presents us with the best option (himself!), then allows us to decide what we'll do.

What will you do?

OVERTIME CHALLENGE

(150 points)

- Proverbs 28:14. What happens to the hard-hearted man?
- Proverbs 28:26. What is the best way to walk in wisdom?
- Psalm 118:8. Who can you trust most?

PRAY IT UP

Dear heavenly Father, trusting in you makes a lot of sense, but it's not easy. It's so tempting to just do things my own way. But I want the best way, Lord, not my way. Show me what it means to lean on you, and be patient with me as I try to do it. Amen.

Bonus Puzzle #4

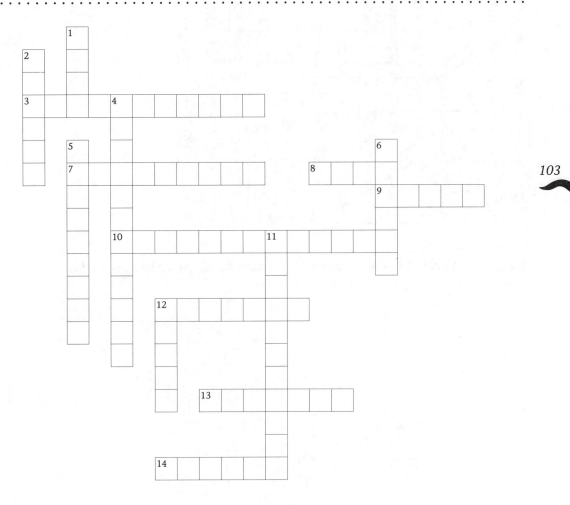

ACROSS

3 "Like a city whose walls are broken down is a man who lacks ___-___" (Prov. 25:28)

7 Don't be too proud to ___ with lowly people (Rom. 12:16)

8 You should never be ___ in your own eyes (Prov. 26:12)

9 "A man's own ___ ruins his life" (Prov. 19:3)

10 "Trust in the Lord with all your heart and lean not on your own ___" (Prov. 3:5)

12 "He who ___ his heart will fall into trouble" (Prov. 28:14)

13 What awaits a stingy man? (Prov. 28:22)

14 "Let another ___ you, not your own lips" (Prov. 27:2)

DOWN

1 There's more hope for a ___ than someone who speaks in haste. (Prov. 29:20)

2 "He who walks in ___ will be kept safe" (Prov. 28:26)

4 There are ___ for not taking responsibility for your mistakes (Acts 5:1-11)

5 ___ was rewarded for taking responsibility for his mistakes (Luke 19:8-9)

6 "It is better to take ___ in the Lord than to trust in men" (Psa. 118:8)

11 "In all your ways acknowledge him, and he will make your paths straight" (Prov. 3:6)

12 If we are ___, we'll miss the way (Prov. 19:2)

Bonus Puzzle #1—Answers to word search, page 31

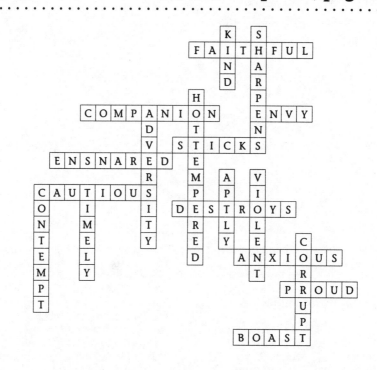

R A S S U R A N C E P W Q E
R O R A Z E T I F E N E B I
R P U D E R E C N I S A L T
E B U C O N Q U E R O R S E
V C O C X S T R A E H Y N S
E F G H E A R T A C H E T T
N A T R U I S H E N L K N I
W I E R E A P A L W E J B N
E T R R T Y L S P V B E G
I F O U F F E E E P V O O
G H U L E S S O X A E C O
H F B H W J M F V E H J Y D
E U L Q U A D R A K I O A
D L E C A E D R A K I O M B
B T N E G I L I D I C T

104

Bonus Puzzle #2—Answers to crossword puzzle, page 55

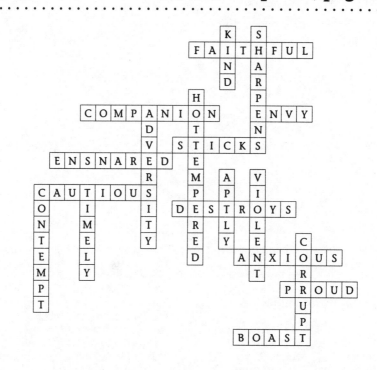

Bonus Puzzle # 3—Answers to word search, page 79

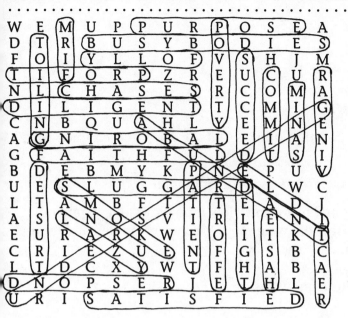

Bonus Puzzle #4—Answers to crossword puzzle, page 103

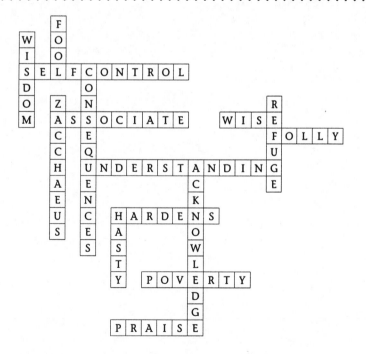

I'd like to hear from you!

1. If you have a "What If" situation that applies better to a certain chapter, write it out and send it.

2. If you thought up different (better?) prizes, write and tell me.

3. Was the book too long? too short? just right? How long did it take you to do this book with your child(ren)? How old were they? Were any chapters too tough? too easy? Send a brief evaluation.

Send your responses to any of these questions to:

Greg Johnson
c/o Tyndale House Publishers
P.O. Box 80
Wheaton, IL 60189-0080